HOW TO SURVIVE THE SEEMINGLY IMPOSSIBLE:
JUGGLING, MAGIC TRICKS, ILLUSIONS, AND OTHER FEATS YOU REALLY CAN DO

by Robin Epstein

SCHOLASTIC INC.

New York Toronto London Auckland Sydney
Mexico City New Delhi Hong Kong Buenos Aires

ISBN: 0-439-57903-1

Design: Julie Mullarkey Gnoy
Illustrations: Kelly Kennedy

Copyright © 2004 by Scholastic Inc.

12 11 10 9 8 7 6   5 6 7 8 9/(

Printed in the U.S.A.

First Scholastic printing, April 2004

CONTENTS

Don't bother! You're never going to be able to do it, so don't waste your time. Give up!

If you're the type of person who doesn't like challenges, stop right now. If you're someone who, after seeing something that looks difficult, throws your hands up and says, "not for me," turn back. If you're the kind of kid who isn't interested in learning secret tricks or super cool ways to solve problems, close this book immediately!

But...if you're the type of person who has banned the word "can't" from your vocabulary, who finds creative problem-solving not only rewarding but *really* fun, and if you love to do things when others insist they're impossible, then this book is totally for you!

How to Survive the Seemingly Impossible is a book that's all about using your brain, your body, and a little something the French call "savoir-faire" (pronounced *sav-wa-fare*, which literally means "to know how to do") to accomplish improbable feats of genius and dexterity. See that? You're only on the first page of the book, and you're already speaking French!

This book is designed to help explain some of the awesome things you sometimes see others doing that you'd like to be able to accomplish yourself. Take **juggling**, for instance. If you've ever seen street performers tossing balls, pins, or fruit in the air, they can almost make it seem easy. But if you've ever then gone home and tried to do it yourself, you probably wound up getting beaned in the head with a poorly tossed banana. In this book, you'll learn how to break things down, step by step, so that with some **patience** and **practice**, you'll be throwing and catching, throwing and catching, and throwing and catching all sorts of objects into the air and then back into your hands again with ease!

You'll also learn how to do some prestidigitation (pronounced *press-tih-dih-jah-tay-shun*) to amaze your friends. In fact, just by using the word "prestidigitation" (which means "sleight of hand" or how you use your hands to trick your audience), you may amaze them anyway! If your goal is to get them to wonder, "how did you do that?" or "where the heck did it go?" you'll want to check out three other sections: **CARD TRICKS**, **ROPE TRICKS**, and **COIN TRICKS**. When magic tricks and illusions are done properly, your audience—either one other person or a whole group—will (hopefully) be surprised, amused, and amazed by your ability to pull the wool right over their eyes.

Just when you're convinced you can figure anything out, solve any problem that comes your way, and beat any odds, you'll find a bunch of deceptively simple tasks that will be utterly impossible to accomplish. That section's called, **"Totally, Utterly, Disturbingly Impossible!"** Sure, it might not *sound* hard to pick up a penny, or catch a falling dollar bill, but you'll see that, when put in certain situations, your body is physically incapable of performing some of the easiest tasks. Don't believe it? We don't blame you—'cause we also like to believe that anything's possible, if you put your mind to it—but try it and see for yourself!

And finally, this book also includes a section called **"Totally, Utterly, Disturbingly Possible!"** which is devoted to showing you how to do very cool things that, by all accounts, logic, and reason shouldn't work—yet you're going to make them happen! You'll wind up doing everything from putting a hole in your hand to making your arms defy gravity—so take that Sir Isaac Newton!

Along with this survival guide, this month's How To Survive Anything gadgets include:

✔ Juggling Beanbags

✔ Deck of Cards

✔ Magic Rope

Juggling: Two Hands, Three Beanbags

Ah, juggling. It's one of those activities that most people think is so difficult that they use it to say things like: "My schedule is so crazy, I have to *juggle* everything to fit it all in." Or, "If I can *juggle* my homework, band practice, and household chores, maybe I'll be able to get to the game after all." Or, "If I can just manage to *juggle* better, maybe I'll have time to breathe...."

Juggling sure seems hard, doesn't it? And the fact that some people can do it so easily can make it even more frustrating!

But the truth is, these "master jugglers" can't help making it look easy, because guess what? It actually IS easy! If you can toss a ball and catch it, **you can juggle!** All you need is to learn the tricks of the trade.

It doesn't take a genius to know that when you throw things up, they're going to fall down, but surely there's *some* genius to figuring out how to make those objects come down *when* and *where* you want them to, right? Well, it turns out this has everything to do with "hand-eye coordination." And if you've ever played a video game, you know how important it is to master this critical skill. Most video games rely on your ability to keep your eye on a moving target, and respond in time to take the right action when necessary.

Your hand-eye coordination skills are probably already pretty sharp. But just like an athlete who's excellent at running the hundred-yard dash, if she wants to do well running another distance, she's still going to have to practice. So the good news is, you're probably already in great shape in your ability to follow moving objects and react to them quickly, and now, the better news is, you're about to become even more expert at it!

Are you ready?

GETTING STARTED

Grab all three of your juggling bags. Roll them around in your hands. Get a sense of how they feel. Picture yourself sending all three bags in a giant loop around your body. Now imagine juggling them through a ring of fire. Imagine that these bags morph into a watermelon, a water balloon, and a puppy, and you're still able to send them in circles above your head. You're now juggling chairs, glass pitchers, and a computer monitor, while you're hop-scotching through your house....

Okay, okay, now come back to planet Earth!

First thing you need to do is put down two of the juggling bags. In fact, just drop them to the ground. (You can think of this as a warm-up for your dropping skills— probably something you'll be doing a lot of at first!)

FIRST THINGS FIRST – USING ONE BEANBAG

Put that bag right in the center of your palm. Don't hold on to it with your fingertips, just cradle it in the middle of your hand, letting the bag rest there for a moment. Now extend your other hand, keeping both elbows close to your body around waist high. Since your hands are now properly positioned, it's time to make your first toss and catch.

Think about tossing the bag from hand to hand, as if you're throwing it over a rainbow, with its highest point at eye level. With light, easy tosses, send the bag back and forth from hand to hand, trying to arc it over the same-sized rainbow each time. Though this step probably seems really easy, it's the foundation of juggling, so you want to make sure you're really good at it before you move to the next step. Keep making those tosses, until they all look pretty similar, going back and forth at the same height and with the same speed. Juggling one bag is the equivalent of learning to walk before you can run, so make sure you're totally comfortable with it; otherwise, you'll end up leaping, lunging, and falling all over the place in later steps.

Next step: **KEEP PRACTICING.** Toss that bag again and again and again. Don't be afraid to do this, like, a thousand times. Okay, you don't have to do it a *thousand* times, but you should do it a lot, got it?

Okay, now you've got the bag rolling, so to speak! So let's keep going and add another beanbag to the mix.

DOUBLE BAG IT, PLEASE!

Remember we just said that tossing *one* bag from one hand to the other was the *foundation* of juggling? Well, if you think of it in the same way, then tossing *two* bags back and forth is the *ground* floor. Using two bags makes juggling start to look like juggling, instead of just looking like you're holding a hot potato in your hands.

Before you start this next step, take a look at the pictures below to help you visualize what's going to happen here. And even before you begin tossing the bags, remember that if they wind up on the ground, you can tell people you're simply practicing your dropping skills!

Here we go....

Pick up two bags and hold one in each hand, keeping them cupped in the center of your palms. Exhale deeply and clear your head. (This won't actually help you juggle, but it's good to do this every now and again anyway!) Now toss one bag up and towards the second hand like last time, but *this* time, when you see that the bag has come to the top of its arc and has begun to fall, toss the bag in the second hand up in the same way, sending it to the first hand. Got it?

No problem, just think about it this way:

1. Toss bag in right hand

2. Wait a second

3. Toss bag in left hand

4. Catch first bag in left hand

Note:
The kid in these pictures is facing you to make it easy for you to follow him. But don't let it confuse you if you've noticed that your right hand is really his left and his left is really your right.

5. Catch second bag in right hand

Still don't have it? Totally normal. This is to be expected and that's why you need to practice. Your hands, eyes, and brain just have to get used to the idea of making the tosses and catches at the same time. It's probably not going to be second nature to you right away…in fact, it'll probably be more like third, fourth, or fifth nature. **But DON'T SWEAT IT!** If you practice this for about a half hour, you'll definitely see and feel a difference. (If only playing the piano was this easy!)

If you're like most people, when you're doing these tosses and catches, you probably always start throwing the first bag from the hand you write with, or your *dominant* hand. And that makes a lot of sense, because you're used to relying on this hand to get the job done. If you've ever tried using a pair of scissors with your other hand, you've realized how awkward and out of shape it is compared to your writing hand. (Unless, of course, you're one of the lucky few people who are **ambidextrous**, meaning you can use *both* hands just as easily. It's a pretty cool trait to be born with—after all, ambidextrous people can write just as easily with either hand.)

But, if you aren't ambidextrous, chances are you've been relying on your dominant hand to learn how to juggle. So take a few minutes and begin tossing the bag in your other hand first, then throwing the bag to your dominant hand. Though it's exactly the same motion and skill, it'll probably still take a bit of getting used to. (The brain can be stubborn that way!)

Wait a minute…you're not cheating are you? You might even be doing this unintentionally by *passing* one of the bags from hand to hand, while *tossing* the other. Before you move on, you *have* to make sure that you're not accidentally taking the easy way out here. There are a couple of ways to cheat in juggling, but just like cheating on a test at school, it's not going to help you learn what you need to know!

Most people don't cheat at juggling on purpose—it probably just happens because their brains are freaking out a bit. **The brain panics when it realizes that one bag is about to land and the other bag hasn't been sent into the air yet.** So its reaction is to try to make up the time by handing the second bag off in more of a pass than a throw.

So you've got to **keep practicing** to make sure you're not cheating, and once you're certain you've got the tosses happening evenly between the two bags, you'll be good to go. And the bags are flying at the same height and width, right? Good, just checking!

Okay…but what if the bags *still* aren't making perfect arcs that land exactly in the palms of your hands? What if you toss a bag into the air and it goes flying across the room? You're probably getting more exercise chasing after those bags than you've gotten all year in gym class! Do your stupid beanbags appear to have minds of their own? Well, if so, the key is putting mind over matter—your mind, that is, over beanbag matter!

Take your bags over to a wall and face the corner. No, this is *not* a sneaky way to punish you, this is just a way of teaching those bags a lesson. Stand far enough away from the wall that you'll be able to move your hands around freely in front of you, but no further away than the length of your leg. Now start tossing and catching the bags. Hopefully, this will prevent the bags from flying in different directions. Sure, you may still not be able to catch them after every time you do a toss, but at least the wall will fence those babies in a little bit!

If you don't like the idea of facing a corner, though, try simply sitting in a chair and doing the tosses while seated. The idea here is **the more relaxed you are, the less wild your tosses are going to be**, so if you're sitting, hopefully you'll be comfortable enough to calm down your hands and brain somewhat.

At this point, we're going to assume you've mastered the two-bag toss and you're ready to move on. But be honest with yourself here. If you're not comfortable, stop for a little while, rest, relax, and come back to it later. Sometimes these things just need to sink in for a while.

TRIPLE IT!

If you're good to go, it's time to do something crazy. That's right, you guessed it: *time for you to walk on water.*

Just kidding! We're not doing anything nearly that hard: we're just going to teach you how to juggle three bags. And guess what, even though it *looks* like it's crazy complicated to master this final step—like it's level 79 on your favorite video game—it's *exactly* what you've been doing already! There's nothing new here in terms of your technique. You're simply going to keep tossing, waiting for one bag to cross the top of the rainbow and start dropping before you send the bag in your other hand in the opposite direction.

Sure, you can argue that this step is MUCH more difficult because now you have *three* bags and you still only have *two* hands, but *GET OVER IT!* Thing is, you're just going to be holding one extra bag in one hand, no big whoop. Still don't believe it? Well go ahead and try it!

Put two bags in one hand and one bag in the other hand. See? Not so hard!

Let's start simple: we're going to repeat the two-bag toss that you perfected in the last section, but now you're going to be holding that third bag in your hand so you can get the feel of it.

Go ahead and toss one of the bags in the two-bag hand up and over—make sure your arc stays at eye level—and as soon as it starts to fall, toss the bag in your second hand. It'll feel a little different this time, because you're trying to hold on to the third bag as well, without dropping it. But it won't be too hard to get the hang of this pretty quickly.

Great, you're almost 100% there—**now you just need to add in the third bag and you'll be juggling!** Take a look at the pictures below to help you visualize what's going to happen in this next step.

The truth is, you already know how to do this, but because your eyes will see more flying objects pass in front of them, they're going to send a message back to your brain that everything has gone completely nutzo! Your eyes will try to convince you that you've got to act faster, toss harder, and snatch those bags up any which way you can. But don't buy into this—you've already been practicing the steps, and if you can **stay calm, cool, and collected**, you'll be doing yourself a HUGE favor.

Okay, you're ready to begin circling those three bags. Look at the pictures below (or check back on page 15)—the bags are numbered to make it easier for you to follow. First, hold two bags (bags 1 and 3) in one hand and one bag (bag 2) in the other hand. Start with the hand holding two bags and toss one over (bag 1). Once bag 1 peaks, throw the bag that you have in your other hand (bag 2). Catch bag 1. By this time, bag 2 should have peaked, so toss over the bag that's still in the hand you started with (bag 3). Right after you toss bag 3, you should catch bag 2. Finally, catch bag 3.

If you followed all the steps and managed to toss and catch the three bags, congrats! You have the basic idea of three-bag juggling down. Now all you have to remember is that this pattern repeats itself, except the hand holding two bags switches sides each time you complete the pattern once. To start the pattern again, all you have to do is toss one bag from the hand holding two bags. But eventually, when you start juggling continuously, you shouldn't be holding more than one bag in each hand at any time—one bag should always be in the air!

Ready? Steady? (take another quick peek at the illustration, then…)

Juggle!

After watching people botch the three-bag toss multiple times (and messing it up ourselves more times than we'd like to admit!), we think we've figured out one of the major problem spots that throws people off. Timing each throw properly is really important, so you want to make sure you're sending each bag into the air at exactly the right moment. If you don't, your coordination will get messed up, and most likely the bags will hit the ground faster than a lead balloon. So, **to make sure you don't send the bags into the air too early or too late, as you toss a bag up, try saying the word "arc."** As soon as you've finished saying "arc", the bag you just threw should have reached the top of its arc. So now toss up the bag in your other hand and say the word "arc" again. When you've gotten the second "arc" out, throw your third bag up and say the word "arc" again. In other words, as you toss each bag, say the word "arc"—and don't throw the next bag until you've finished saying it. If someone happens to walk by, they should hear something like this: *"Arc. Arc. Arc. Arc. Arc. Arc. Arc. Arc. Arc."* So, with each "arc," toss a bag!

Once you get going, you'll want to instantly juggle all three bags for hours without dropping them, but chances are, that's not going to happen. (If by some chance it *does*, call the folks at the Guinness World Records™ because you're clearly some sort of amazing juggling whiz!) For the rest of us mere mortals, juggling requires much more practice in order to get the hang of it. Don't worry, you'll totally be able to get it eventually, if you keep at it— just rest assured that this isn't something that's necessarily second nature to all of us.

So what should you do? Um, how about PRACTICE? THEN PRACTICE SOME MORE. THEN PRACTICE SOME MORE. THEN SOME MORE. THEN SOME MORE!!!

Now you may get tired. You may get frustrated. You may get sore (and we mean both kinds of "sore" like the *angry* sore and the *physically* sore from having to pick up all those fallen bags). None of this is unusual, it happens to the best of us. What you want to do, in this case, is **take a little break**. Maybe a *long* break. If it's not coming right this very moment, sometimes there's nothing better you can do than to stop doing it for a little while and try it again later. We're willing to bet that once you come back and start trying it again, after you've rested a little, you'll be much better at it!

EXTRA FUN

To take a break from three-bag juggling, why not juggle your three bags with a friend?

When you've lined up a partner, the two of you should stand side by side. For an easy warm-up, we'll start with two bags. Each of you should have one bag in your outside hand—the hand that's furthest away from the other person. Now tell your partner to toss his bag "over the rainbow" and towards your hand. As soon as his bag hits the peak of the arc and starts to fall, you should send the bag in your hand up and over to his hand, as you're about to catch his bag. Throw your bag in a way that goes just inside his arc, so neither one of you has to go leaping for a catch.

Once you get good at exchanging the bags back and forth without much difficulty (and hopefully without hitting each other in the head too often!), introduce the third bag into this exercise.

Have faith, **you can do it!**

To juggle three bags with your partner, stand side by side again, but this time, have your partner hold two bags in his outside hand while you still hold one. Have your partner get the party started by tossing you his first bag. Once it has arced, you should toss your bag over to him. Once your bag peaks, have him send over the other one he's still got in his hand, and shoot the one you just caught back to him after his second bag arcs. Keep doing it. And again. And again!

And remember, the best part about **two-person juggling** is that, if the balls keep hitting the ground, now you have someone *else* to blame (and help you pick them up)!

Good work! Can you see how you've gotten all the moves down?

Now, when your partner gets tired or you think you're ready to try three-bag juggling by yourself again, thank the person who was just helping you, then give it another shot on your own.

Remember, stay relaxed and focused!

Toss, catch, toss, catch, toss...guess what? You're juggling! You probably just dropped all the bags you had in the air at this fantastic realization, didn't you? Well, that's no big deal because now you know that when you pick the bags back up, you'll know exactly what to do with them!

You should keep in mind that even the best jugglers eventually drop the things they have up in the air—gravity makes sure of this. So if anybody else is watching and you drop everything, just tell them you did it on purpose, to add a little dramatic flair to your show (and to fool them)!

Once you get really good at juggling your three bags, you can start substituting the bags for other objects, like fruit. Small apples are usually a good bet, since they're not much bigger than your beanbags, and if they fall, they won't bust apart and leave a huge mess on the floor!

How about tangerines?

How about turkey drumsticks?

A flamingo? Well, probably not such a good idea....

Think you can master grapefruits? They're definitely going to be harder, since they're probably bigger than your hands, but if you're in the zone, give it a shot.

Look around your house and try to find other objects that you might juggle. Once you get really good, you won't even need to use three objects of exactly the same size. For instance you could use, say, a bar of soap, a harmonica, and a scarf.

Be creative! You're only limited by your imagination…okay, and to be totally honest, also by your ability to juggle…but once you've mastered the task, it'll be just like riding a bicycle. You'll never forget how to do it—and you'll probably even have a hard time remembering what life was like *before* you knew how!

Footbagging: Just for Kicks

You might not believe this, but there's an entirely different use for those little beanbags—one that has actually become a sport that's played internationally. It has worldwide competitions, as well as international club associations, and it's known as *footbagging*, but you might be more familiar with the American name for it: **Hacky Sack**.

Hacky Sack History

The game was created in Oregon City, Oregon, in 1972, when two friends started kicking around a handmade beanbag. They called their game "Hack the Sack," and they designed special "Hacky Sack" beanbags. Within a few years, footbagging had become a favorite alternative sport, sprouting up in parks, on college campuses, and wherever people had itchy feet and the desire to hack together.

Want to give it a try? This is a great activity to get others involved in, too, so eventually you might want to ask some friends to join you. With others you can do "freestyle footbagging," which basically means kicking the bag around the circle and doing various tricks. But first, it's probably best to play around with one of your beanbags alone, so that you get the feel for what you're doing.

RULES OF THE GAME

Before you get started, there are a few basic rules you should familiarize yourself with.

- The primary thing you need to keep in mind is that the game is called *footbag* because it doesn't involve the hands or arms at all—except when you're first getting the bag into play.

- If you're footbagging with other people, being courteous to your "playmates" is key. Even if you're much better at keeping the bag airborne than the other folks in your circle, you can't just hog the bag to yourself. After you've done your kick, make sure you send the bag in the direction of someone else. If you only want to play by yourself, that's a whole different ball of beans, but once you've invited someone to play with you, you've got to make them feel welcome in your circle by giving them their turn.

- When playing footbag, EVERYONE is going to make mistakes. Everyone is likely to drop the bag, kick something they didn't mean to, send the bag flying in an odd direction—you get the idea. It's understood that everyone messes up, so no one has to say "I'm sorry."**

(**Okay, you can say you're sorry if you *really*, *really* want to, but unless you've done serious damage to something or someone, people know you're still in the learning process.)

WHERE TO PLAY AND WHAT TO WEAR

Since your feet are such a big part of successful hacking, it's worth it to discuss the best surfaces to play on and the best footwear to be playing in.

Grounded

Generally it's a good idea to start a footbagging freestyle circle in an area where the ground is packed dirt, like on part of a field where the grass has worn away. Why? Well, sometimes grass can hide holes or dips in the ground. Since this is a sport that requires a lot of fast footwork,

23

you don't want to risk tripping or falling. You might think footbagging on pavement would be a good idea, and you wouldn't be totally wrong. But, since it's likely that (especially at the beginning) your beanbag is going to be hitting the ground a fair amount, pavement can be rough on the bag itself, and leave ugly scrapes on its surface.

Shoes Clues

You want to go with some type of sneaker that fits really well and gives you a full range of motion, like a cross trainer.

BASIC MOVES

There are four basic moves that you'll probably want to get down if you're hoping to become an expert footbagger. All of these moves will require practice, so don't get frustrated if you can't master them immediately. They are:

1. Inside Kick **2.** Outside Kick **3.** Knee Kick **4.** Toe Kick

INSIDE KICK

Hold the bag waist high and drop it. As it falls, cross your foot up in front of you and hit the bag with the inside or insole of your foot. (The insole is the area on the big-toe side of the foot, where the arch is the highest.) Repeat this move a bunch of times, since this is one of the key moves in playing the game.

OUTSIDE KICK

Sometimes when the bag is coming at you from an odd direction, or when you want to send it back to another person, you'll want to employ the "outside kick" technique. The best way to achieve it is to bring the foot up and out to the side, then move it back in the direction of your butt. Your foot should be lifted and hit the bag when it's waist high. Between the height and the sweeping motion of your foot, it should give the bag a bit of a spin when you send it off to the next person.

KNEE KICK

The knee is key, especially when you're footbagging by yourself. Bring your knee up as if you're about to climb a low stair step. Hold the bag about waist high and drop it over your knee. As soon as you let go of the bag, lift your knee towards it in a fluid motion. The bag should bounce off your knee, probably moving a bit forward, so you can either hit it again with your knee or your toe.

TOE KICK

The toe kick requires a good eye and good timing. It's not difficult, but it takes practice to know the best time to hit the bag. When doing the toe kick, make sure your ankle is relaxed, and almost limp. To practice, hold the bag about waist high and drop it over your foot. Lift your foot to "kick" the bag, but make sure you connect your toe with the bag—not just the end of your foot—so that you can achieve the maximum flick-back effect.

Once you get the basic moves down, keep practicing, so you can figure out how to control where you kick the bag and how fast it goes. But one of the great things about the sport of footbagging is that "anything goes". Almost any move you can think of to return the bag is considered "fair," so don't be afraid to use any and all creative body movements to keep that bag in the air!

AWESOME! Now you can juggle with your beanbags *and* play hacky sack. But, guess what? There are still LOADS of other things you can do with your beanbags!

You can use one of the bags as a doorstop

You can use it as a paperweight

You can use it as a hand and finger "flexer"

You can use it as a pillow to rest your head against your desk

What else can you use the beanbags for?

Make a list and see how many things you can come up with. If you can get ten, that's pretty good. Twenty-five and we'll be mighty impressed. And if you come up with over fifty uses for these beanbags, we might even offer you a job!

Card Tricks: Deal with It!

F or some awesome tricks and cool magic to delight yourself and to entertain your friends, all you'll need is your **How To Survive Anything deck of cards** and a couple of people in the audience.

THE SUPER CARD SHUFFLE

GET READY TO RIFFLE!

Before any card trick gets started, you'll want to shuffle the deck thoroughly so your audience is certain you haven't messed with the cards in any way (you know, set them up in a particular order or placed one card in a specific part of the deck). Don't worry, eventually you WILL be messing with cards JUST LIKE THAT, but when you start the trick, you want your audience to believe everything is normal! So, learning how to shuffle the deck well will make you look like a real pro (and give the audience confidence in you).

One of the most basic shuffling techniques (that looks really cool and makes an excellent sound, too) is called the *riffle shuffle*. It's one of those card-handling basics that you'll want to do well, and it's a cinch to work once you've practiced it a few times.

So first, grab your deck and "square" it— this means making sure all of the cards are together in an orderly fashion and that no random edges are sticking out. You can either square the cards in your hands, or you can bang the deck on one edge, against any hard surface, like a table.

Put the pack in your right hand, and put your thumb on one of the shorter edges, and your other fingers—every one EXCEPT the pointer finger—on the opposite short edge. Take your pointer finger, bend it at the knuckle, then rest it against the back of the deck, just like you see in the picture.

Now, with the palm of your left hand facing up, bring it towards the bottom short edge of the deck in your right hand, like you're about to catch the cards if they fall. And now you're ready to riffle!

What the heck is a *riffle*, you ask? No, it's not a ridged potato chip, and the dictionary actually lists a couple of definitions for it. But for our purposes, it means to flip or "thumb" through, to "ruffle" or manipulate something between the fingers.

To get a good riffle going, what you'll first want to do is bend the pack backwards a little. Your pointer finger will help you, if you push the nail on that finger into the back of the deck. You should notice that the deck bends slightly. Now let her rip, or riff, as the case happens to be! Let the thumb release about half of the cards from the deck into the palm of your left hand, which is already in position to catch them.

Good! Now square the two halves of the deck, and put your hands back on both half decks, like you just had them in your right hand above (thumb on one side, every finger but the pointer on the other, the pointer bent and pressed against the back of the deck). Make sure the half decks are facing each other. Now turn each half of the cards down, almost bringing your thumbs together in the middle. You can rest the fingers on the opposite side of the deck against a table, if you want. Press your pointer fingers into each half to make the cards bend slightly.

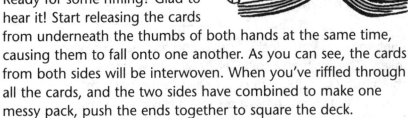

Ready for some riffling? Glad to hear it! Start releasing the cards from underneath the thumbs of both hands at the same time, causing them to fall onto one another. As you can see, the cards from both sides will be interwoven. When you've riffled through all the cards, and the two sides have combined to make one messy pack, push the ends together to square the deck.

And that's it! You've just done a complete riffle shuffle. Most professional card handlers do the riffle shuffle a few times in a row, and do it very quickly, so it looks like the cards always stay in motion, and that they're thoroughly mixed up. So you should try to do it a few times, too.

RIFFING ON THE RIFFLE

If you want to add a little pizzazz to the riffle shuffle, you can add on a different way to end it, sometimes called a "bridge." Basically, to do the bridge, you want to do the shuffle exactly the way you just did it UNTIL you get to the point at the end where you're pushing the two sides of the deck together. For this little trick, don't push the ends in as a way of squaring the deck. Instead, place your thumbs in the middle of the cards and curl the rest of your fingers under the left and right sides, respectively.

Use those fingers to bend the cards up (causing your thumbs to lift slightly and to make the cards into the shape of a rainbow). Now, let the tension go—and watch and listen as the cards re-combine once more!

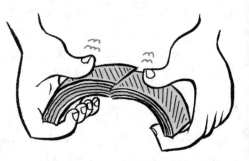

Look through your deck of cards and find both of your jokers. They're pretty spiffy, eh? Okay, now throw them out. (All right, you don't have to throw them out, just put them somewhere else.) Having the jokers in your card deck while doing these tricks can mess up your magic (no joke!), so it's best to put them aside.

CAN'T GET YOU OFF OF MY MIND....

This first card trick should astonish your audience, simply by using the power in your head.

What you're going to do is pick your volunteer's card out of the deck by making it stick to your forehead, which impresses an audience, not only by making them believe you magically knew which card the volunteer picked, but it also wows them because they'll start thinking your forehead is as sticky as fly-paper!

HAIR POLICE

The one thing you need to do before you get started is to pull back any hair that's hanging over your forehead. So if you have bangs, just use a bobby pin to hold them back, or use some hair gel. Whatever you do, just make sure that your forehead is balder than a bald eagle!

SHOW TIME

Shuffle your deck of cards thoroughly in front of the audience, so that they're convinced you haven't stacked the deck in a particular order. Call a volunteer up and hold the deck of cards out in your hand fanned out. Make sure to keep the back of the cards facing you, and the front of the cards (the sides with the suits on them) facing the audience. Make a big deal about the fact that you obviously can't tell which cards are which. Say something like:

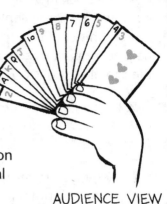

AUDIENCE VIEW

> *"As you can see, I can't see any of the cards, and since you just saw me shuffle them, you know I have no idea where any particular card landed in the deck."*

Now tell your volunteer to choose any card he wants from the deck and have him show it around to the other members of the audience (if there *are* other members of the audience, that is!). Then say:

> *"And whatever you do, DON'T let me see what card you've chosen!"*

As he's flashing the card around the audience, you should divide the rest of the deck in half. Put one half in your right hand, the other half in your left hand. You'll want to say something like:

> *"Promise me you won't forget what card you've chosen, okay? Got it? Good. Now I want you to put that card right back into the deck."*

31

Hold the stack in your left hand out towards your volunteer so he can add his card to it, making sure he places his card face down on the top of that deck. Then say:

MAGICIAN'S LEFT HAND

VOLUNTEER

"Now we'll put the cards back together, so that your card is lost in the deck."

BUT…what you're really going to do is to take the deck that you have in your right hand and place it on top of the stack in your

MAGICIAN'S VIEW

left, making sure that the stack from the right is placed about an inch below the stack from the left. Picture it this way: if your left palm is facing up, when you add the cards from your right hand on top of the ones already in your left, you'll want to make sure that the left-hand stack is still peeking out about an inch on the top near your fingertips.

Now, you have all the cards in your left hand?

Okay, good, next step: tilt the cards away from you. The top stack will slide forward somewhat and cover the top edge that was peeking out. However, the card that was on the very bottom of

the top stack (the deck from your right hand) will stick out slightly. That's your key card—it's not the volunteer's card, but it's what's known as the "marker"—and it's going to help you keep track of your volunteer's card, which is directly below it! So it's important to keep it sticking out a little.

MARKER CARD

MAGICIAN'S VIEW

Slip Sliding Away

The "slide" is the trickiest and most important step of this illusion to master, so you'll probably want to practice it a couple of times. Because you don't want your audience to realize that you're creating a "marker" card, you need to do this as smoothly (and in a way that attracts the least amount of attention) as possible. To practice, keep cutting (or dividing) the deck in half, and take one half in your right hand and the other half in your left. So you know you're doing it correctly, take a look at the top card in the deck on the left (which is your volunteer's card), and the bottom card in the deck on the right (which would be your marker card).

Now place the deck in the right hand on top of the one in the left, making sure to place it about an inch below the deck on the left. Tilt your hand away from you and see what happens. Is that marker card sticking out a bit? Awesome! If it isn't working, keep practicing, and eventually the force (gravity and friction!) will be with you.

Now that your marker card is set, you need to tell the audience that you're going to cut the deck again. Go ahead, play this up:

MARKER CARD

"Behold! I will now cut the deck!"

Using your empty right hand, take a small number of cards from the TOP of the deck and put them down on a table in front of you. Remember, don't lose track of that marker card—keep it sticking out a little so you know where to find the selected card below it. Now tell the audience that you're going to cut the deck AGAIN.

"And to make sure that your card is truly lost in the deck, I will cut the cards once more."

But this time when you're cutting the deck, you want to take ALL the cards from the top up to and INCLUDING your famous marker card. Put this stack on top of the others you just laid down.

(At this point, your volunteer's card will be the top one in the deck you're still holding in your left hand.) Announce to your audience that you're going to mix the decks one more time, just to show them everything here is on the up and up—of course what's really going to be on the "up and up" is the selected card, which will now be at the top of the stack!

"Here we go, one final time,
just for good luck!"

VOLUNTEER CARD ON TOP

Put the cards in your left hand on top of the stack on the table and bang the whole deck against the table, to make sure the cards are squared up.

Of course, you know that the selected card is now at the top of the deck, but the audience should have NO IDEA. The key to the next few steps is to make them believe you really don't have any clue where that card is, and that it will take unbelievable powers of mentalism for you to be able to figure it out. Tell the audience that you think the cards are trying to speak to you, to tell you the right answer.

"Wait a minute, did you hear that? You didn't? Well I did…
I think the cards are attempting to communicate with me.
There they go again—don't tell me you didn't hear that! No?
Really? Okay, well they told me that I needed to clear my mind,
so I could better receive their signals."

While you're doing this, lick the tips of your fingers and wipe a little spit on the back of that top card on the deck (the volunteer's card!). Then quickly lick your fingers again, and rub them into your forehead, as if you're massaging your head.

Now close your eyes and put your forehead directly down on top of that deck. You'll want to press your forehead pretty firmly on the deck because you're trying to get the card to attach itself to your forehead. You can keep talking to the audience, telling them that you're beginning to see things a little more clearly now.

"Yes, yes, it's coming to me...I'm starting to zone in on the card, I can almost feel it now."

Next thing you want to do is double-check that the card is, in fact, sticking to your forehead, so you'll want to lift your head up a few inches off the table, without letting the audience see that you've got anything attached yet. If the card isn't sticking, quickly wet your fingertips again and add a little more spit to the mix.

Now with your head still parallel to the table, and with the selected card stuck to your forehead, take the rest of the deck and start spreading it out in front of you. Tell the audience that you can practically "feel" the right card.

"I think if I just put my mind to it, I'll definitely have it in another few seconds."

Keep pretending you're searching for that card with your hands for a few more seconds, then say, "Voila!" and lift your head up, showing the audience that the right card is now anchored to your forehead.

As they laugh and clap in amazement, you tell them:

"I'm just stuck on being right!"

FEET DON'T FAIL ME NOW!

You've used your head, now it's time to use your feet!

Think you can cut cards like a chimp? Our distant relative, the great ape, is almost equally good at doing things with his hands and his feet. So if you're up for a little monkey business, you can amaze your audience by showing them how you've got magic down to your tippy toes!

With a little help from our friend Science, we're totally going to pull a fast one on your friends. All you need is your deck of cards, a smooth floor, a few pinches of salt, a pair of loose-fitting pants with pockets, and your clean, sweet feet (getting those babies to smell nice, now *that's* what we call magic!).

Before you get this trick going—and before you're in front of your audience, you'll want to put a few pinches of salt in your right-pant pocket. (Don't be stingy, but don't use up the whole saltshaker either!) Now take your deck of cards and ask your volunteer to put it down on the floor, anywhere he wants to.

"I want you to take this deck of cards and place them on the ground, wherever you think best."

(It's always a good idea to let your audience believe they have control...suckers!) While he's doing this, put your hands in your pockets and make sure you've got the salt ready to go.

VOLUNTEER

MAGICIAN

Tell your volunteer to cut the deck in half and to take the top half of the pack and fan those cards out on another part of the floor. He can place them near or far from the other half of the pack, it doesn't really matter. After he's spread out those cards, tell him to choose a card from that pile. While he's choosing it, quickly lick the tips of the thumb and index finger on your right hand (assuming you put the salt in your right pocket. If you're a lefty, and put the salt on the left side, then lick those fingers on your left hand). You don't have to wet these fingers thoroughly, you can just run them past your lips, as if you've got a hair in your mouth or something, because you just want them wet enough so that some grains of salt will stick to them when you put your hands back in your pocket.

While you're telling your volunteer to study his card, put your wetted fingers into your pocket and rub some salt on them.

"Now I need you to look at that card very carefully, memorize it, and study it the way you would a winning lottery ticket. Got it? Good, now put it on top of the other half of the deck."

You can gesture with your foot towards the other half deck of cards (the ones not fanned out). Once he's put his card on top, tell him to square the other deck back up because he's going to combine the two packs so that his card will be lost in the middle of the deck.

"Please straighten up the fanned-out cards now and put them back on top of your card. This way you can be sure I won't know where your card is in the middle of the deck. And just to be sure I'm not getting any strange signals, straighten up the fanned-out cards so that there aren't any pointy edges or things sticking out that might help me find it."

Here's the deal: while your volunteer is busy straightening the other half deck of cards, and you're gesturing to the pack that has his selected card on top, you'll need to drop some of the grains of salt on it. Rub your middle finger against your thumb and let the salt drop on the volunteer's card. (You want to make sure you get a decent amount on there—about a pinch worth—because the salt is going to help the other cards roll off it.)

SALT

Don't worry, your volunteer's not going to see you do this because he's busy straightening up the other half deck. (But if you have an audience of more than your volunteer, don't make it too obvious.) Now tell the volunteer to place that deck on top of the pack containing his card. As you know, the salt is going to mark the spot, so you're all set to perform your "feat" of magic!

"Thank you. And now it's time for these piggies to go to the market."

Now gently kick the deck with the side of your foot (just like in the picture) and as they're spreading out, say:

"Apparently this little piggie wants to come all the way home to his mommy."

The deck will separate the most where you put the grains of salt, so you'll be able to identify your volunteer's card—because it'll be the one right after the big gap. Pick that card up (and you'll probably be able to see or feel a few of the granules of salt left) and show it to your audience, telling them:

"I call that no small 'feet' of magic."

Note: if you've got really big feet (or if this deck is really small), you might want to try this trick with bigger cards.

VOLUNTEER'S CARD

THE GOTCHA GAME!

This next card trick is especially fun because just when the audience starts to doubt your amazing skills, you use the ace up your sleeve, so to speak, and show them who's got the magic!

The secret to this trick is being able to see and remember what the bottom card in the deck is. So once you've got that down, you'll be ready to thrill and amaze. All you need is your handy dandy deck of cards and a volunteer.

Tell your volunteer to give the cards a good shuffle, so he'll know there's no way for you to know their order. After he's finished shuffling them, quickly fan them out, face side up, and show them to him.

MAGICIAN'S VIEW

KEY CARD

> *"Take a look at these cards. Do you agree that they're well-shuffled and there's no way I could remember what order they're in?"*

(You can even turn your head away from the deck while he's examining the cards, so he won't accuse you of trying to memorize the order. *As if!*)

Meanwhile, the ONLY card you need to worry about looking at is the one that's now at the very top of the deck. (Since it was the one originally at the bottom, when you flipped over the deck to fan it out, the bottom card temporarily became the top card.)

Now put that deck back down again, making sure the card you just memorized is back on the BOTTOM of the deck. Ask your volunteer to cut the cards and to take the top half of cards and put it on the table (we'll refer to this as the Left Deck). Tell him that he should now take the top card from the other pack of cards (which we'll call the Right Deck) and look at it carefully. (Remember, even though we're going to call them Left Deck and Right Deck here, it's important that you don't refer to them that way while you're performing the trick because an audience member might catch on.)

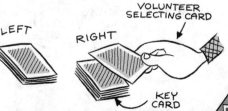

LEFT

RIGHT

VOLUNTEER SELECTING CARD

KEY CARD

"Please take the top card from this stack right here and study it very carefully, but don't show it to me. Repeat: don't show it to me because this is your special card."

Now instruct the person to put his special card on top of the Left Deck. Okay, here's where you're about to get sneaky. Tell the volunteer that you want him to feel very certain that his card is going to go right back into the middle of the deck, so you won't have any idea where it is. Therefore, he should now re-combine the two packs of cards by

placing the Right Deck on top of the Left Deck. You know, though, that the bottom card you memorized on the Right Deck is now sitting directly on top of his card in the Left Deck.

Ask your volunteer to cut the whole deck again, then re-combine the cards. If you have another volunteer, tell him to cut it, too.

Now take the whole deck in your hand, with the backs showing, and start dealing the cards. This means, take every card from the top of the deck and flip it over to show its face as you lay it on the table. Make sure you tell the volunteer who selected the card not to say anything or make any facial gesture that could tip you off in any way when he sees his card come up. Keep dealing the cards out, until you see your special card (the one that was the original bottom card). You know that the card immediately following the key card in the deck is going to be your volunteer's card, but you'll want to play it cool and pretend like you don't know this yet.

So, deal out your volunteer's card, then deal a few others after that, too. Your volunteer is going to assume you missed seeing his card, since you've already gone past it. And now you should say:

VOLUNTEER'S CARD   KEY CARD

"Yes, ladies and gentlemen, the next card that I turn over from this deck will be the card specially chosen by my volunteer here."

The volunteer may start shaking his head, he may start laughing at you or saying, "no, no, no." But instead of dealing the next card from the deck, you're going to pull his card out from the ones already on the table!

To finish off the effect, take the volunteer's card and "turn it over," placing it face down on the table. That way you can end the trick by saying:

"See that?! I told you the next card I was going to 'turn over' was going to be yours!"

Note: if you're doing this trick and you find that the key card (the one that was originally at the bottom of the deck) is the last card that you deal out (instead of being in the middle of the deck), don't panic! That just means your volunteer's card was the first one you dealt out.

Knot It! Mastering the Trick Rope and the Rope Trick

You've sent juggling beanbags flying through the air and you've wowed your audience with your card-handling skills. So now that your hands, eyes, and ability to deceive are in proper working order, it's time to learn a few new tricks so you'll never find yourself at the end of your rope!

Rope is an essential prop in every illusionist's toolbox. So the more you "know the ropes," the more you can make them work to your advantage!

Here are some great rope tricks to try:

THAT'S SEW COOL!

Rope comes in all shapes and sizes, but when you're first learning to handle it, regardless of its size or shape, it's still difficult to control. For instance, if you've ever used very thin rope—like thread—you know how hard it can be to manipulate that, too. As a matter of fact, few things can seem more frustrating than trying to get a thread through the tiny eye of a needle. But with this next trick, you'll show your audience that even a person with the shakiest of hands can get a very large piece of thread through a very small hole. Ready to shock and amaze?

Good!

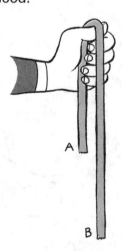

Now grab that rope, partner, and hold it in your left hand so that about five inches is hanging down below your fist. This short part of the rope, we're going to call "end A". The longer part of the rope that's sticking out at the top by your thumb, we'll call "end B".

"If any of you have ever tried threading a needle, you know how hard it is. As a matter of fact, getting that thread through on the first attempt is practically a trick in itself."

Now stick your left thumb out a bit and, with your right hand, start winding the rope from end B towards you, so it first goes over the thumb, then under it, then back over.

Wind that end around your thumb as many times as your thumb will allow (just remember not to wrap it *too* tightly because the purpose of this trick is not to strangle your most important digit!).

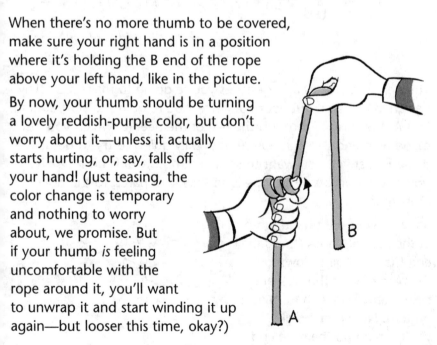

"Excuse me while I prepare my sewing equipment."

When there's no more thumb to be covered, make sure your right hand is in a position where it's holding the B end of the rope above your left hand, like in the picture.

By now, your thumb should be turning a lovely reddish-purple color, but don't worry about it—unless it actually starts hurting, or, say, falls off your hand! (Just teasing, the color change is temporary and nothing to worry about, we promise. But if your thumb *is* feeling uncomfortable with the rope around it, you'll want to unwrap it and start winding it up again—but looser this time, okay?)

Now, with your right hand, make a loop in the top part of end B. If you imagine a real needle, this loop represents its "eye." It doesn't really matter what size your loop is, but the smaller you make it, the more people will doubt that you'll be able to complete the trick—which is always a good thing!

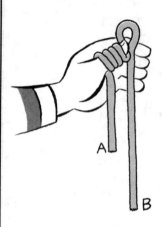

"Okay, now you can observe how I have created the eye of the needle. Yes, that's right, keep your eyes fixed on this eye."

Now, hold that rope in a loop between your left thumb (the totally wrapped-up left thumb) and the pointer finger on your left hand. Press the thumb against your palm to prevent the loop from coming undone, as you release your left fingers.

"Compared to the width of my rope, the eye of this needle is very small."

The next few moves and gestures you're going to make are solely designed to psych out your audience. You're going to start aiming end A (the thread) through the eye of the needle (which you just made with end B)—but you're not really going to try to get it through just yet. You want to show them how difficult a task it's going to be because the rope is so thick compared to the hole it must fit through.

So, with your right hand, grab hold of the rope at end A (that's the end that's hanging down by the base of your thumb), and hold it about an inch from its bottom. Now pretend like you're lining up the rope end with the eye of the needle, and move the "rope thread" back and forth a few times to make it look like you're doing a few practice takes to figure out how to thread it through. Do this slowly so that the audience will realize how difficult it's going to be for you.

> *"Next time I do this trick, I'm going to lay off the caffeine beforehand so my hand isn't so shaky! Okay, here we go..."*

Now, count to three (and you can have your audience count to three for you, if you'd like), and start loosening the grip on the loop in your left hand a little. Next, take end A and aim it to the right of the loop—and you can shoot it as close to or as far away from the loop as you want—just make sure you pull that end across the area between the left thumb and the left pointer finger.

MAKE NO ATTEMPT actually to put the end of the rope through the loop! On the count of "three," quickly thrust end A out towards your audience to the right of that loop.

Be sure to pull the rope to the right of the loop.

Amazingly, you have just managed to "thread the needle" without getting the thread anywhere near the eye itself!

> *"As you can see, I'm a whiz with a needle and thread, but the funny thing is, I still can't sew buttons!"*

Sew-duh!
There's now one less turn of the rope wrapped around your left thumb because each time you "thread" the needle, you use up some of its length. So now you know how the trick works!

KNOT THERE ANYMORE

You just magically pulled a rope through the eye of a needle; now it's time to learn how to make a knot disappear.

Just follow these easy directions, and **your friends will be stunned when you tie a knot in the middle of your rope, and then, just by pulling at its ends, you'll make that knot vanish into thin air!**

First thing you need to do is show your audience the rope you're going to use. Let them examine it, hold it, bite it, whatever they want to do to make sure they feel confident that you're not using any sort of trick thread or anything. Now take an end of the rope in each hand, and again, we'll refer to the rope in your left hand as end A and the rope in your right hand as end B.

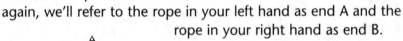

Take your right hand, which is holding end B, around the back of your left hand and place end B between your pointer and middle fingers. Make sure end B is crossed over the top of end A. You can now move your right hand away, so you'll be ready to use it in the next step.

Okay, good, now take your right hand and slide it through the hanging loop of rope. (Your hand should move straight out and away from you.) Then take end A (which is the part that's sticking up as the top part of the cross) and grab onto it with the thumb and pointer finger of your right hand.

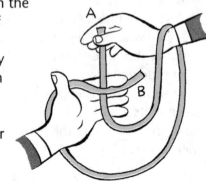

What you need to do next is to pull apart the two ends of rope, so grasp end B with your left thumb and pointer finger. (End A is still being held by the thumb and pointer finger on your right hand.) Now pull end A back through the loop and hold it there.

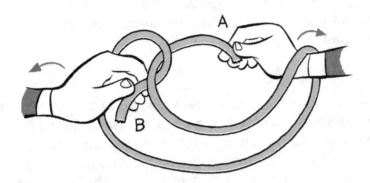

As you should now be able to see, you've managed to create a loose or "fake" knot in the center of your rope. You need to do a little work here, so that it doesn't fall out before the trick is done. Since this knot is false, you need to stiffen it a little by twirling the ends towards you as you pull your hands apart. Look at the arrows on the picture to see what we mean!

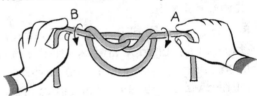

It's a good idea to twist the rope like this, because when the rope gets rolled, the knot in the middle is able to keep its shape, since it's basically sliding up and over on itself. The more you twist, the tighter the knot will look.

But then…just when it appears that the knot is about to become a permanent fixture in the middle of your rope, tell your audience that, with your breath, you'll be able to knock out the knot. As you blow, pull on the ends of the rope and, quicker than the blink of an eye, that "knot" will no longer exist. In other words, you can tell your audience:

"Knot so anymore!"

Since you just made a knot disappear in the last trick, it's practically a law of nature that you need to make one appear in the next one!

THAT'S KNOT NUTS

Tease your audience by showing them how **you can put a knot in your rope without letting go of the ends**...and don't worry, we're not asking you to tie the knot with your feet! (Although we'd be *very* impressed if you could do that.) As you may have guessed, there's a trick involved that's the key to this whole illusion, and if you cross your heart and promise to practice, we'll tell you what it is.

Okay, did you do it? Did you cross your heart? If so, congratulations! You've already mastered the trick to this trick. That's right, the key to this illusion is to make sure you cross your arms before you get started doing it.

But first, you're going to want to bring up a volunteer so he can check out your rope and assure the other audience members that it isn't rigged. As soon as you've got your volunteer up with you, let him watch you tie a knot in the regular way. Demonstrate a basic "overhand knot." All you have to do to make this knot is to take the two ends in your hands, cross the ends over each other, then pull one of the ends through the loop. Once you've pulled it tight, you've got it! Couldn't be easier, right?

> "As you can see from this demonstration, putting a knot in this rope isn't very difficult, is it?"

Of course, your volunteer will respond, "no, it isn't hard at all," or something like that. Now ask your volunteer if he thinks he can put a knot in the rope.

> *"You look pretty handy, think you can put a knot in this rope?" (Wait for your volunteer to answer "yes," then say:) "Okay, but there's one catch. I want you to tie the knot without letting either one of its ends go. So, you have to tie it without letting your hands leave the rope, okay?"*

Presumably, your volunteer still won't think that's too hard a task, but boy-oh-boy, that's where he's wrong. Unless he's a master contortionist who's capable of bending his body in all sorts of ways, he's not going to be able to do it...but definitely let him attempt it! (Make sure he keeps both hands on the rope the whole time, otherwise he'll be able to tie that knot and your trick won't carry the same punch.)

When your volunteer has become totally exhausted and given up, or you've grown tired of making fun of him, tell him you'll show him how it's done.

> *"Well, gee, I'm not really sure why you were having such trouble with this. Really, it's very simple."*

Lay the rope out on a table. Extend your left arm out in front of you, then grab that elbow with your right hand. Now take your left hand and tuck it over your right arm and under the right elbow, so that your arms are crossed over your chest. Your volunteer is going to figure out that he's been fooled, so you might as well let him in on the gag at this point.

"You just need to grab that rope just like I've done."

What you want to do now is pick up the left side of the rope with your right hand and the right side of your rope in your left hand. You need to make sure one of your hands (the right one) is picking up that rope as it's crossed over your arms, and the other hand (your left hand) is picking up the rope underneath and through the bottom of the elbow crook. Best way to do this is to bend forward slightly and twist your body a little bit. Take a look at the picture above, if you're not getting it right away.

Now stand back up and you'll have some extra rope in a U-shape below your arms, and you'll be holding onto the rope with both hands.

"And now to amaze and embarrass you…One…Two…Three!"

At the count of three, uncross your arms, slowly pulling them to their normal sides of the body, while still holding on to the ends of the rope. As you do this, you and everyone else watching will see that you've made a knot appear in the rope, while keeping both hands on it at all times!

Funny Money: The Art of Coin and Dollar-Bill Tricks

If you ever hang around adults, you'll often hear them talking about money. They'll say things like, "Money doesn't grow on trees, you know," and "If I had a nickel for every time I heard that excuse, I'd be rich!" Well, with these great tricks, you'll be able to convince them that you can make money appear and disappear faster than a shopper on a buying binge at the local mall. So if you're tired of hearing grown-ups complain that making money is hard work, tell them you can prove them wrong with this simple trick.

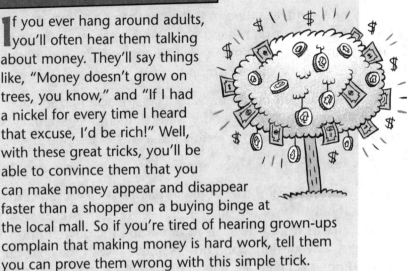

CAN'T HEAR YOU, I'VE GOT A QUARTER IN MY EAR!

Pulling change out of someone's ear is a trick that's been around forever. Why? Because everyone likes to think they have something valuable in their heads! *(Ha, ha!)* With this illusion, you can tell your friends you're going to start turning their thoughts into cold, hard cash. Of course, you're not *really* going to convert a brain into a piggy bank. What you'll actually be doing is hiding the coin in your palm the whole time, but with your skilled magician's hands, you can make it *look* like you've snatched a quarter right out of someone's ear!

All you'll need to get started is some sort of coin. (We suggest using a quarter because it's a nice size for you to hold on to, and big enough for your audience to see. But if you can't come up with the 25 cents, you can use a nickel, dime, or penny. You'll also need a volunteer. So ask your audience if anyone is willing to help you out.)

"For my next stunt, I'll need a volunteer ear. Come to think of it, I'll take a volunteer who has two ears, just to give me a little extra to work with in case something goes terribly wrong with this trick!"

With your volunteer sitting in a chair next to you, start by holding the quarter in your right hand with the tips of your first three fingers (and by that we mean your thumb, pointer, and middle fingers). Show the quarter around to the crowd.

Now hold your left hand out, with its palm facing up so your audience can see that it's empty, and tell them they should watch closely because money frequently has a way of disappearing:

"As you know, money can often slip through your fingers."

Move your right hand over your left palm to make it look like you're about to drop the quarter into it. **Here's where you start your critical fake out.** Instead of putting the quarter into your left palm, as your right hand hovers above it with the coin, curl up all the fingers on your left palm just to make it *look* like they're grabbing hold of the coin. In other words, just *pretend* to be dropping the quarter into your left hand!

What those fingers are actually doing is helping to hide the quarter and fingertips of your right hand.

The key to this trick is that your audience mustn't be able to see that the quarter has remained in your right hand the whole time, so you want to make very sure that your left hand is covering the right, as its fingers curl up. While the audience is watching what's going on with your left hand, slide the quarter into your right palm with the thumb. Once the quarter is in position, ball up your left hand (like you're holding the quarter) in a fist and move your hands apart. Remember, the faster you do this move, the more convinced your audience will be that nothing fishy is going on!

THUMB HIDING QUARTER IN PALM

To keep the audience's attention focused on your left hand, keep your eyes on that hand. You'd be surprised, but just by looking at your left hand, those watching you will also think that's where the quarter is.

Since no one is paying attention to your right hand now, bring it down to your right side as casually as possible. Remember, you're trying to keep everyone's eyes away from your right hand, so it's important to be cool about this step. Meanwhile, ask your volunteer to blow some magic wind on your left hand. (Before he does it though, remind him you said to "blow" on your hand, not spit on it!)

Once the "magic wind" has been blown, open up your left hand and reveal that the quarter has disappeared! Thank your volunteer by saying:

"Look, I don't mean to suggest you NEED a mint, but that breath of yours seems to have melted my quarter!"

Now take a moment and start examining one of your volunteer's ears. Don't use your hands yet, but start looking at the ear from all angles, making it seem like he's got something fishy in there.

QUARTER

BEHIND VIEW

"Wait a minute, wait a minute! I've heard of wanting to keep your money in a safe place, but this is ridiculous!"

Move your right hand close to the person's ear, and with your thumb, slide the quarter back from your palm into your fingertips. Let the quarter gently touch the tip of your volunteer's ear so he actually believes something is coming out of it, then pull your right hand back. Hold your hand up, with the quarter in your fingertips, and flash it around for your whole audience to see.

Now you can turn back to your audience, point to your volunteer and say:

"If he ever tries to get out of paying a bill by telling you he's 'not made of money,' just tell him to give his head a little shake and see what happens!"

Mission accomplished. Good work! You probably noticed that the hardest part about the trick is actually mastering the fake out at the beginning. Therefore, it's a good idea to practice it in a mirror until you can do it smoothly and quickly. After all, if you can make yourself believe you've put the quarter in your left hand while still keeping it in the right, your audience will be fooled, too!

DOUBLE OR NOTHING

Now that you're a cash flow pro, here's another way to dazzle, using your digits. Have you ever heard of quarter jumps? No, not one-fourth of a jump, but actually a quarter that jumps from hand to hand? You haven't?

Well, that's because there's no such thing...BUT...you're about to make it look like there is! So when you show this trick to your family and friends, you'll have them believing you can make a quarter jump better than a Mexican jumping bean!

What you're going to be doing in this illusion is somewhat similar to the "vanish" you pulled off in the old "quarter-from-the-ear" routine. The key part of that trick is the same as the key in this one: you're going to make the audience believe you've passed a quarter from one hand to another when, in fact, you'll simply keep the quarter in the original hand it started out in.

In order for you to do this new illusion, though, you're going to have to up the stakes a little...in other words you're going to need to get another quarter! Or, if you can't get your hands on two quarters, you can always use another type of coin. You just need to make sure whichever type of coin you go with, you've got another one of the same kind.

First thing you want to do is set your two quarters (or coins) next to one another on a flat surface where your audience can see them. Now pick one of the quarters up in your right hand and hold it in your first three fingers (the three starting with the thumb).

"Behold, a magical quarter. That's right, with this and
$5 you can get a cup of hot chocolate nowadays."

And here comes the fake out: bring your right hand over towards your left hand. The left palm is open and facing up to show your audience that nothing's hidden in there. Then, make it look like you're placing the quarter into that palm by starting to curl up the fingers on your left hand. Of course, what you're really doing is sliding that quarter back up and into your right palm with your right thumb, while making the audience believe the action is taking place in your left hand. Remember, for this to look real, you've got to make the left-hand-grab look as convincing as possible.

THUMB HIDING QUARTER IN PALM

Hold that left hand closed like you're protecting something very valuable— not air! Now move your left hand away from your right hand, and again, watch it so the audience thinks that's where the magic's taking place.

HIDDEN QUARTER IN RIGHT HAND

AUDIENCE VIEW

"Do you know where a snowman keeps his money?
A snow bank!"

Your nimble fingers are going to help you here in this next step because now you need to pick up that second quarter on the table in your right hand, without letting anyone see that it still contains the first quarter. Practice this pick-up a few times because it's harder than you think! Remember, your thumb can't help you lift it, since it's still holding the first quarter against your palm.

Once you've managed to get that second quarter into your hand (without letting the two coins jingle against one another), curl your right hand up so that both your hands are in fists.

HIDDEN QUARTERS IN RIGHT HAND

AUDIENCE VIEW

"Now I want you to watch these magical quarters as they go leaping through the air."

Here's where you get to add a little razzle-dazzle to your trick. Hold both fists up in the air, making sure to keep them closed. Wave them around. Shake them one at a time like they contain lucky dice. Now bring your lips close to the wrist of your curled left hand and blow across it like you're opening your fingers with your breath. Open up that left hand and show the audience that there's absolutely nothing in there!

LEFT HAND

"And it's gone! Boy, a quarter may not be worth much these days, but this is ridiculous. But hang on a second because I think I've found a way to double your money...."

Now go ahead and open your right palm, revealing the two quarters and proving that you've managed to make one quarter magically jump through the air and into your fist!

HIDDEN QUARTERS IN RIGHT HAND

RIGHT HAND

WHEN IT COMES TO MONEY... USE YOUR HEAD!

One thing people love is "easy" money, right? So if you tell them they have the opportunity to make some in this next trick, chances are you'll have so many volunteers, they'll trip over each other to get up to the stage. Tell your volunteer that if she can simply catch the quarter you're going to drop three times in a row, she can keep your pocket change. Sure sounds easy, doesn't it?

Seems like your volunteer will be going home with your hard-earned quarter...well, not if you use your head!

As you'll see in this trick, by using your head as a hiding place, you'll not only impress your friends by making them believe you've vanished the quarter, you'll also make certain they don't go home with any of your allowance!

All you need is one regular quarter to get started, and, of course, a money-hungry volunteer.

Note: for this trick to work, you either need to be taller than your volunteer, or if not, be sure to have a chair so your volunteer can sit while you stand.

THERE'S GOT TO BE COINS AROUND HERE SOMEWHERE

Now, lay out the rules for your volunteer:

"Okay, in order for you to keep this quarter, all you have to do is catch it three times in a row. Ready?"

Now tell your volunteer to open her hands and get ready to catch, as you take the quarter between your thumb, pointer, and middle fingers and hold it slightly above your head. Explain that the volunteer can stand or sit wherever she'd like, to give her the best chance of catching the quarter.

"Here it comes!"

From the position above your head, gently drop the coin into the person's hands, making it very easy to catch. Basically, you want her to think that this is going to be the easiest 25 cents she's ever made. Take the quarter back and raise it above your head again. But before you hold it out to let the coin drop, let your hand scrape the top of your head for an instant, almost making it look like you're fixing your hair a little before you do the drop.

(This step is just paving the way for the fake out in the all-important "third drop" step.)

"You caught the quarter very easily the first time, let's see if you can do it again!"

Release the coin from your hand and let it drop right back into your volunteer's palm. Again, make it easy so the person really thinks she's got the hang of it. Take the quarter back and start lifting it over your head again, again pretending like you're fixing your hair. But this time, before you extend your arm fully, **slip the quarter onto the top of your head** without letting anyone see you've done this, then lift your hand up into the position you had it in for the past two drops. Even though you're not holding the quarter anymore, you still need to make it *look* like you are, so you'll want to make sure you keep your fingers pinched together like before. And also remember to keep your head up straight so the quarter doesn't slide off while you're doing the trick!

"Okay, you're now very close to pocketing my change. You just need to catch the quarter just this one last time."

Now make it look like you're dropping the quarter, and watch your volunteer move to catch it. She'll soon realize that the quarter has vanished and that, somehow, you've pulled a fast one. You can then tell her that you'll be able to make the quarter reappear, but only if she agrees that all bets are off. As soon as she says "yes," have her get into catching position as you lift your hand to the place where you've done the drop from each time before. When she's ready, make it look like you're dropping the quarter from your hand, but really just tilt your head forward so the quarter can slide off of it.

"Well, you know what they say, you almost had it, but the money just slipped through your fingers!"

TOE JAM!

Have you heard of the once-popular shoe style known as the Penny Loafer? Those shoes were cool because, built into the top, there was a little space where you could hold a penny or two. Though the Penny Loafer is somewhat out of fashion these days, it's never a bad idea to keep some change on hand, even if it means using your foot! Read on to find out how!

How many times have you found a lucky penny on the street?

Even if the coin itself didn't bring extra luck, it was lucky just finding it, right? Well, the answer to that is "yes" and "no". Though it may have been good luck for *you*, it was bad luck for the person who lost it! The luck from a "lucky penny" all depends on which side of the coin you're looking at.

Hopefully, if you lose a coin one day, you'll find another at some point soon. Often it seems like there's loose change everywhere—on the ground, between the couch cushions, at the bottom of a book bag—people drop coins all over the place. But in this next trick, you'll see that keeping your coins on the floor is one of the best ways of hiding them in plain sight!

So far you've used your hands a lot to pull off some pretty cool tricks, but now it's literally time to put your best foot forward and get those tootsies into the action.

To do this trick you just need a small coin—try using a penny or a dime—**and your favorite pair of sneakers** (or any other type of shoe for that matter!). To start the trick, you're going to do something that looks much more klutzy than cool—you're going to drop your coin on the floor. Of course, you don't want anyone to think you've done this on purpose, so you'll want to make it look like an accident.

"And for my next trick...whoops!" (drop the coin)
"I better get that because it's never too early to start saving up for college!"

Move very close to the coin so it's right in front of your right foot. Try to make this look natural, as though you're simply positioning yourself to make picking up the coin easier. Next, start bending over to pick it up while you continue talking to the audience.

> *"Just like that old saying, 'a penny saved is a penny earned,' right?"*

But here's the trick: instead of actually picking up the coin, you're going to slide it under your shoe! It takes some practice to do this without having the audience see you, so be very careful to follow these instructions.

As you're bending, bring your right hand in front of your right leg, and keep the back of your hand facing the audience. When your hand gets to the ground, it'll basically block the audience's view of

the coin. Now *pretend* like you're picking up the coin, as you also slightly lift up the toe of your right shoe. (To make this trick look really good, practice the coin pick-up part before you start. The better you mime picking up a coin, the more convincing you'll be, so just to get the feel of it, bend over and pick up a coin. Keep doing this action until you get the feel of how much your knees actually bend and what scooping the coin into the tips of your fingers looks like.)

Quickly slide the coin underneath your right shoe and casually put your toes back on the ground, before anyone sees.

Meanwhile, keep talking to the audience. The more they're concentrating on what you're

saying, the less they're focusing on what you're doing down there on the ground.

"Sometimes these little things are hard to get a handle on. Then again, I usually don't have a problem getting my hands on money—it's holding on to it that I need help with!"

Now stand up and make it look like you've got the coin in your right hand. You don't need to make a fist this time, but just show the audience the back of your hand. This way, you make them believe you're actually holding on to the coin with your forefingers and thumb when, in fact, your hand is totally empty.

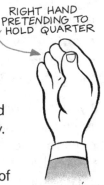

RIGHT HAND PRETENDING TO HOLD QUARTER

MAGICIAN'S VIEW

A great way to tease the audience is to keep looking at your right hand throughout the rest of the trick because they'll assume, wherever your eyes are, the coin is. Poor suckers don't realize that the coin has stayed in *exactly* the same place on the ground. Be sure not to tip them off by looking down towards your shoe. If you *do*, their eyes will follow!

AUDIENCE VIEW

Okay, now you're going to tell the audience that it's time to perform a great feat of magic. You're going to make the coin disappear! Move your right hand towards your left and make it look like you're simply swapping the coin into your left hand. Now that it looks like you have a hold of it, ball the left hand into a fist.

"Hey, wait a second! Something's a little fishy here."

Open your left hand first and reveal that there's nothing inside it, then open your right hand—and holy moly—you'll reveal that there's nothing in that hand, either!

"Told you I had a hard time holding on to my money!"

You can end this trick in two different ways. You can either pretend that the coin has magically reappeared under your foot:

"Well would you look at this...(lift up your foot and reveal the coin) I always heard that money is a stepping stone to success, but I never thought I should take that literally!"

WELL, WOULD YOU LOOK AT THIS!

Or, if you have some double-sided tape, before you start the trick, you can put some of it on the bottom of your right shoe—attach it at the top of the sole by the toes. But if you don't have that kind of tape, the regular stuff will work just fine, too. All you'll have to do is make it into a loop, sticking one of the edges onto the end of the other (and remember to keep the sticky side facing out!). When you're doing the trick and sliding the coin under your shoe, make sure the coin is under the part with the tape. That way, when you walk away after the illusion is complete, there's no evidence of the vanished coin. (If you're using tape, it's best to do this trick on a hard floor or sidewalk—carpet will pull the tape off, and your audience won't be fooled a bit!)

TAPE LOOP

You've now learned how to fool an audience by making them believe you can send coins to seemingly impossible places. But now it's time to become skilled at a trick that harnesses the power of science for the purpose of a prank!

Do You Think You Can Pass a Quarter Through a Dime-sized Hole?

Grab a quarter and a dime. Take a look at them carefully. What do you see? Two silver-colored coins, right? But there's also a pretty obvious difference between the coins aside from how much gum they'll buy you, and that, of course, is their size. The dime is a relative shrimp in comparison to the whale of the quarter. Even the little nickel, which is worth only five cents, is much bigger than the ten-cent piece.

Now, considering the fact that the quarter is much bigger than the dime, if you saw a paper with a hole the size of a dime cut out of it, you'd probably assume there's no way the quarter could fall through it, right? Seems pretty clear that, unless you rip up that paper pretty well, the quarter just can't squeeze through a hole that small, true?

FALSE!

This little trick is a great one to bet on with your friends. Tell them you'll bet your quarter that you'll be able to slide it through a regular sheet of paper that simply has a hole cut out of it the size of a dime.

The key to this trick is that it involves a little 3-D action. You're literally going to turn the flat piece of paper (which is normally considered two-dimensional) into something three-dimensional, by folding it on the diagonal—but we're getting ahead of ourselves a bit.

The first thing that you'll need to do is line up your props: a quarter, a dime, a sheet of paper, a pen, and a pair of scissors.

Trace the outline of the dime onto the middle of the paper, then cut the circle out. To show your audience that there's NO way the quarter can fall through a hole that small, put the quarter directly on top of the hole, and hold the paper by its edges so they can see it. You can even show them that it's impossible to shove the quarter through the hole, by trying to fit it in that way (but be careful not to rip the paper while you're doing this).

Now what you want to do is to fold the paper diagonally (bring the bottom left corner towards the top right corner) across the center of the hole so it looks like a half-moon. Slide the quarter inside the crease and let it drop towards the hole. It should poke out a little bit on its own. Now what you want to do is pull up on the outward edges of the paper crease and jiggle it a little bit. With a bit of manipulation, the quarter will fall right out of that little dime hole.

DIME
SIZED
HOLE

QUARTER

If your friends ask you how this worked, you can explain that, by folding the circle in half, you've distorted the shape into an ellipse (or an oval). An ellipse looks different than a circle, but with a bit of squeezing and stretching, they can be made into the same thing. In this case, there's a short diameter and a long diameter, so when you fold the circle into an ellipse and put the quarter through it by pulling up on the shape's edges, you're actually sliding the coin through the shape's long diameter.

DOLLAR DAZE...

This is going to be your most expensive trick yet, because in order to do it, you've got to get your hands on two dollar bills. No, not one two-dollar bill, but two one-dollar bills. Got it? Good.

A lot of people are impressed by money by just seeing it, but **in this next trick, you're going to make your audience believe that you have the ability to make your dollars magically pass through one another!** (This type of trick is an optical illusion called an "impossible penetration.") And despite the fact that you really won't be jamming those dollars together, to your audience it'll *look* like you can handle money better than a bank teller!

First, you need to roll those dollar bills up tightly into short tubes, and hold one in the crook of each thumb (between the thumb and pointer finger).

"If you're like me, you want to make sure your money is very secure."

Turn your hands in opposite directions so that the thumb on your left hand is facing downward and the thumb on your right side is facing up. Now take hold of the top part of the tube bill in your left hand with your right thumb, and put your right middle finger at the bottom of that tube. Meanwhile, your left thumb should go to the bottom part of the tube in your right hand, and your left middle finger should go to that tube's top.

"That's why I like to make sure my dollars always stay in one place!"

Now spin your hands in opposite directions as you begin to pull them apart. It's like you're turning your left hand away from you and the right hand towards you. It will look like you just made your dollars pass through one another as you separate your hands!

As you might have guessed, you can do this trick with a variety of other objects, too, like straws, or small pencils. The only thing you want to keep in mind is that you need to be able to keep a firm grasp on the objects between your middle finger and thumb, and you want to make sure the objects are of very similar size and shape.

As you just saw, seeing something with your own two eyes isn't necessarily proof of anything! When our brains receive certain signals, it's known as a "sensation." How the brain interprets these signals is called "perception." When the brain botches its interpretation, an illusion is produced—and an illusion is something that doesn't correspond to what's there.

Totally, Utterly, Disturbingly Impossible!

Hopefully, by now you've realized that with a little practice, there's a ton of cool stuff you can achieve that you previously thought was impossible. And we're really glad that you're no longer looking at things and thinking, *"Who are you kidding?!? I could NEVER do that!"* Or, *"That's way too hard for me, I'll let someone else do it."* **As a general rule, it's stupid to under-estimate yourself. However...**

Occasionally when people tell you something's impossible, they're not kidding around, it really *is* undoable. Once in a while, there will be an impossible feat that NO ONE is going to be able to achieve regardless of how hard anyone tries. For instance, no one has managed to run a mile in under a minute, no one has figured out a way to live without sleeping, and no one can resist a freshly baked chocolate chip cookie...okay, maybe *someone* can do that, but that person clearly has super-human strength.

So if someone dares you to walk on water, you'll probably be smart enough to reject the challenge because you know you would sink like a stone. However, sometimes there are things that sound like they *should* be really easy to accomplish, but they turn out to be utterly undoable—kind of like those math problems you struggle with on exams!

The next few activities are things that at first glance seem really easy, but for one reason or another, turn out to be physically impossible. The good news is, now that you've been clued into the fact that these things physically can't be done, you won't feel like the suckers your volunteers will be when you ask them to perform these "basic" tasks—and they fail over and over again.

DOLLAR DROP...

To start you off on an easy warm-up, we'll have your friend chase something in the air that he *thinks* he'll be able to catch—but can't. All you'll need is a buck, and a friend willing to take you up on a little bet. (Don't worry, you'll win, trust us.)

Ready to make your friend chase after the almighty dollar? Good!

Take that dollar and fold it lengthwise, making a sharp crease in the bill. Grab one end of it with your thumb and pointer finger and find yourself a chump—uh, we mean a volunteer.

Tell your friend that if he can catch the bill when you drop it, it's his to keep. You can even tell him that you'll make it really easy for him to make the money because you're going to let him hold his hand close to the bill. Now instruct him to put his thumb and pointer finger (or thumb, pointer, and middle fingers), close to the bottom of the dollar, just like in the picture here.

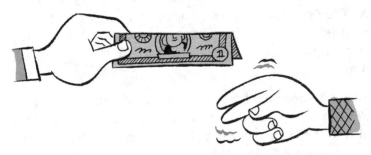

Okay, now drop it!

Your friend blew it, didn't he? He couldn't catch the dollar that was practically right there in his hand. Does this mean that your friend is completely slow and pathetic? Maybe.

Still, that actually has *nothing* to do with why he couldn't catch the bill. Regardless of how quick or good with his hands your friend happens to be, it's still HIGHLY unlikely that he'll be able to grab that descending dollar. And the reason is because most people's reflexes are simply too slow to react in a situation like that. Since the drop happens so quickly, the mechanism in the brain that tells us to catch isn't triggered fast enough.

Usually when something is falling, the brain has enough time to alert the body to spring into action. Take the game of baseball, for instance. When a batter hits the ball and it goes whizzing into the air, even though the action happens quickly, from the time the ball hits the bat to the time the ball flies through the air towards them, the players on the field still have at least a second or two to see where the ball's going, position their gloves, and get ready to catch it. They can miss the catch, of course, but usually if they can get themselves properly aligned, it'll land in their mitts. For this reason, pop flies are usually the easiest type of balls to catch: because they take so much time in flight—first going up, then arcing back down—the player has plenty of time to get into a good position to make the catch.

In the case of this dollar bill, however, **it falls before your friend's brain has time to process what's going on, and to react.** The eyes will see what's happening and send a signal to the brain telling the hands to respond, but even though the body's "instant messaging" system works in under a second, it's still too long.

There's only one person who can actually catch that bill as it falls (and we're not talking about The Flash). It's you, the dropper! It turns out that the body has what's called a "proprioceptive (*pro-pree-oh-sep-tiv*) sense." What that means is that because all the activity is happening within your own body, it's aware of its own movements, and it coordinates its reactions accordingly. While your friend had to wait to see the bill drop before he could begin to respond, since you did the dropping, your hand knows to line up for the catch as soon as you've released it. Therefore you, the dropper, are not reacting to the sight of the flight, just the movement of your "dropping hand." Interestingly, actually seeing the bill fall is what makes a person's reaction time slower!

You've used your fingers to do a lot of amazing stuff so far, but it's time to put the spotlight on your least appreciated digit— your pinky! Maybe your pinky doesn't *look* like it can do much, but in your next trick, it'll be doing *all* the work!

MORE STRENGTH IN YOUR LITTLE PINKY....

It's time once again to prove how much control you have over your buds! So get ready to school your buds by showing them that you can keep 'em down with only your little finger. Just find a willing volunteer and a chair, and you're ready to go!

Have your friend sit in the chair and tell her to keep her head back and her chin up.

"Make yourself comfortable in the chair, but not too comfortable, because you have to keep your chin up and your head back!"

Explain to your volunteer what you're about to do—namely that you intend to keep her stuck to the chair just by using your little finger.

"Now you may not believe me when I tell you this, but I can make your bottom stay in that chair like it's stuck there with super-glue just by using my little pinky!"

Go ahead and press your pinky finger into her forehead. You don't have to apply much pressure, just push in a little bit. Now ask her to try to stand up without moving sideways or wiggling around. Amazingly, as long as your friend follows your directions (and doesn't cheat), she's not going to be able to stand. Naturally she's going to assume you have the world's strongest pinky!

But, as you probably have already figured out, there's a bit of a trick involved. In order for a person to stand up, she needs to position her body in a certain way so that she's able to establish balance. Therefore, the reason your volunteer can't stand up is because, without being permitted to move her head slightly, she's not going to be in the right position to get her balance, and her body won't move. Because your pinky is pressing against her forehead and therefore preventing it from tilting forward, you're stopping her natural movement. Once you've done this, you've effectively frozen her to her seat!

WALL FLOWERS

Common walls. They're everywhere, and chances are you're surrounded by four of them right now! You wouldn't necessarily think of a wall as something that would actively prevent you from doing something, but as it turns out, regular walls can be deceptively difficult objects, despite the fact that they just stand around looking fairly innocent all day long! As you'll see in these next few activities, when you come into contact with a wall, it's going to prevent you from being able to do some of the simplest tasks.

Try this trick out by yourself first, then bet your friends that they won't be able to do it either!

A LITTLE PICK-ME-UP

All you need for this trick is one coin and one wall. As soon as you have those two ingredients, you're ready to…fail!

Stand with your back to the wall, making sure to keep your heels and head against it. Now let your coin drop right in front of your feet.

So far, so good, right? Nothing too hard here. So, if we told you that you won't be able to pick that little coin up off the ground, you'd probably laugh because how hard could it be to pick up a coin, right? But, making sure you keep your heels against the wall, go ahead and try to bend over and pick that coin up. If you don't cheat by moving your feet, you'll see that, before you can manage to get your hands on that coin, you're going to tip like a punching clown.

As long as you keep your heels against the wall, it turns out that

there's NO WAY you can bend over and get that coin without losing your balance first. Your body is strategically weighted and balanced so that your center of gravity is right over your feet. Therefore, if you try to move forward to grab the coin, your center of gravity will start to move forward with you. So in order to maintain balance, your feet have to move forward as well. But if you can't move your feet, you're stuck!

Now that you know the trick and are totally certain that it can't be done, go ahead and get your friends to try it. We're not encouraging you to gamble, but it probably wouldn't be a bad idea to tell them that if they can pick up the coin, you'll clean their room for the next week. But, if for some reason they can't do this INCREDIBLY EASY task, they'll have to clean up *your* room!

NO JUMP SHOT

Stand with your back against the wall. We're just about to prove to you how standing against a wall will prevent you from doing something else really easy, too. This time, however, it has nothing to do with your ability to pick up money from the ground, but **if you keep your back pressed against the wall, you won't be able to jump.**

Go ahead, give the jump a shot. Or give it a jump shot, whatever you prefer!

Aha! Caught you! When you tried to jump, you moved away from the wall, didn't you? We know this because if you did in fact jump, you would have had to have moved your feet, tilted your head forward a little, and let your backside go backwards.

If you really *did* keep your back pressed to the wall, then you really didn't jump. The best you were probably able to do was a little hop.

Amazing, isn't it? Who would have thought such a little action could cause such big problems!

Totally, Utterly, Disturbingly Possible!

So now that we've bombarded you with things you *can't* do, it's time that we show you stuff that you didn't even know you *could* do! Read on to discover how your own body has some cool tricks of its own!

You probably don't spend a lot of time thinking about how amazingly cool, miraculous, and seriously weird your body is. It takes you through the day, surviving harsh conditions, temperature changes, and even the most disgusting school lunches! It performs millions of tasks without ever consciously needing instruction, and does everything from seeing squiggly lines on a page and interpreting them as letters, to making you raid the refrigerator when you need to eat, to the most basic and critical things like breathing and sleeping. If you really stopped to think about all the extraordinary actions your body performs, you'd probably be in awe of it. (Of course, some people *are* awed by their bodies simply when they look at themselves in the mirror…but that's another matter altogether!)

But the human body really *is* amazing. For instance, if you know the answer to a question your teacher asks, you automatically raise your hand, right? You don't first have to think to yourself "Arm, I need you to extend in the air, stay there for a while until I hear my name called, then drop back down." You just raise it and put it down when you need to. It's a learned response that's become second nature.

Yet it turns out that there are a lot of things going on in our bodies that we can't control. As you saw in the last chapter, there are certain simple things you just won't be able to do (and we're not just talking about solving science equations or doing a triple back-flip). But then again, there are other things that will strike you as completely impossible, like, say, **seeing a hole in your hand**, or **making your arms defy gravity** that you'll be able to accomplish easily.

This next section will present you with a variety of illusions and tricks that have everything to do with what they *can* do.

FLY ME TO THE MOON....

Though Wilbur and Orville Wright showed us that it was possible for men to fly, the brothers who were "first in flight" never managed to figure out how to do it without making us sit in an airplane.

But you don't need to fly when you do this next trick because, as you'll see, your arms will look like they're about to take flight on their own! Don't believe us? Well, then by all means, give it a shot!

Stand in a doorway (one where you know no one will bother you or make you move from) and with your fingers pointing towards the floor, push the backs of your hands and wrists against the doorjamb as hard as you can for one minute. After the minute is up, relax your arms and walk through the door without tensing up too much.

What happened? You did the funky chicken, didn't you? Okay, maybe it wasn't the funky chicken *exactly*, but your arms seemed like they floated up, didn't they?

You probably found that you were able to stop your arms from rising once they started moving, but the body's first instinct was for them to continue extending out and up. The reason for this is because your arms were reacting to muscular pressure. By pushing your wrists against the wall, you were activating and tensing the muscles all up and down your arms. When you stopped pushing, those muscles needed a minute to realize they were no longer needed. Because you'd worn them out, they weren't "thinking" clearly. (It's sort of like trying to concentrate in history class, if you haven't gotten a good night's sleep…try as you might, you're still going to be a few steps—or years—behind!)

Hole in One!

Pull out a dollar bill again—you're going to need to prove once more how amazing your body is.

You've got a hole in your hand! Don't believe it, eh? Well we'll prove it to you. Roll your dollar bill horizontally into a long tube. (If you don't have a dollar handy, just take a regular sheet of paper and roll that up into a tube.)

With your right hand, bring the tube up to your right eye so that you can see through it easily. (You want to be very careful when you're doing this though, because if you think getting a paper cut hurts when it slices the tip of your finger, you can only begin to imagine how much it will smart if you accidentally nick your lids!)

Now, close your right eye so that you're only looking out of the left one, and hold your left hand out (with the palm facing you) so that it extends a few inches beyond the end of the tube. Look at it with your left eye. What do you see? Just your regular old palm so far? Good, because if you're seeing something else—like a disgusting green fungus or the traces of your last science project— we'll really have to insist that you stop what you're doing right now so you can go and wash those revolting hands!

Okay, now start moving your left hand closer towards you, but stop moving it when the edge of your hand (just below the pinky) hits the side of the tube. Just to make sure it's in the right place, you can press the edge of your hand against the tube and push it in a little. Got it? Now open your right eye up (so that both eyes are open) and take a look.

TUBE OVER RIGHT EYE

LEFT PALM BESIDE TUBE, FACING YOU

What do you see? By any chance did you discover that you have a giant hole in the middle of your hand?!?

So how is it possible that you located a hole in your hand when you looked at it through a tube? Does the tube possess some sort of amazing X-tra strong X-ray vision? Nope, sorry. (But how cool would it be if it actually did?)

In the most literal way, this trick is an optical illusion. What happens is, that by using the tube, you're forcing each eye to operate separately so they wind up sending different messages to the brain. Your left eye was looking at your left hand and was just seeing the hand, so it communicated that information to the processing centers in your brain. But your right eye—the one that was looking through the tube—was also seeing the round hole at the end of that tube. Therefore, when it sent its official message to the brain, it basically said, "I (or eye) spy a hole!" Even though you've probably got a nice big brain in that head of yours, those two conflicting messages totally confused it. But in an effort to sort out all the facts, the brain decided to synthesize, or combine, those pieces of information, and it wound up making it look like you had a hole in your hand!

We swear it was just an optical illusion and that you really *don't* have a big hole in your palm…but just to be sure, why don't you try washing your hands again just to check?

Of course, not everything that looks strange or impossible to our eyes is an optical illusion—sometimes it's just good old-fashioned fraud, as you'll see in the next trick!

Now That's Twisted!

You've been doing some great work so far, amazing your friends and family, and probably freaking them out with your "extraordinary" abilities. So it's time to reward yourself with a little snack. But before you chow down, let's do another illusion, using one of the world's best finger foods, the mini-pretzel!

To do this trick properly, you're going to need to use a few little pretzels of the knotted variety (unfortunately, the stick or the rod kind won't work).

What you're going to do is break off one of the links in the round upper part of the pretzel. Lick the broken edges (the two at the sides of the snapped-off piece, and the two corners where the piece just came from) until they're moist. Don't drown the pretzel pieces in spit, but make sure they're good and wet.

Now take another one of the mini-pretzels and hook it into the new hole on the broken pretzel. What you need to do next is to reattach the broken piece onto the first pretzel, like you're gluing the handle on a broken tea cup. The only difference is, instead of using glue to fix the problem, you're using spit! To make sure the pretzel edges attach, hold the link in position for a minute or so to let it dry properly. Once it's dried, you shouldn't be able to tell that one pretzel had been broken at all. It should just look like the two pretzels are "permanently" linked together.

You're good to go now, so it's time to bring the audience in. Hold the linked pretzel in your left hand very gently and make sure you're keeping one of the pretzels hidden from the audience's view. Keep your thumb and pointer finger right over the area where the pretzels are linked, and let one pretzel stick up from your hand.

The other pretzel should be hidden in your palm. Don't press too hard on that link, though, because "glue spit" isn't quite as reliable as good old white glue and you don't want the pretzels to come undone. Keep the back of your hand facing the audience, so they can't see what you're holding in your palm.

HIDDEN PRETZEL

LEFT HAND

"Every good magician knows the importance of doing things in a step-by-step order."

Pick up a new pretzel in your right hand and hold it exactly the same way you're holding the linked ones in your left hand; in other words, you want to grasp one of the loops between your thumb and pointer finger.

RIGHT HAND

"Sometimes things get hectic, though, and the best way to bring about order is with a little chaos."

Now toss the single pretzel you're holding in your right hand into your left hand. Practice this a bit, since you'll have to still hold onto the two linked pretzels that are already in your left hand.

When you manage to master the catch, you're going to need to hide that single flying pretzel in the middle of your left palm underneath your pinky, ring, and middle fingers. While you're doing this, scoot the hidden linked pretzel up in your hand and pinch it between your pointer finger and thumb, letting the top pretzel dangle down.

HIDDEN PRETZEL

If you do it right, your audience will think that when you threw the pretzel up and caught it, you managed to link it magically in your hand!

"Now that's what I call bringing about order— at least to the food chain!"

And here's the best part—now you get to pop those linked pretzels in your mouth so that no one will realize you've been spitting on your props!

Running a Little Hot and Cold....

Water, water everywhere! Here's another one of those activities that seems like it should be a no-brainer, but will in fact blow your mind.

You're going to need three bowls, and you want to fill them with water of different temperatures. One bowl should have cool, refrigerated water. The second bowl should have water that's warm. And the third bowl should have hot water (you don't want it to be boiling, you just want it to be like hot-shower-water temperature).

Line up those bowls and put the one with warm water in the center. Now put your right hand in the cold water and your left hand in the hot water. Let your hands stay there for three minutes. At the end of that time, lift your hands up, and without bothering to dry them off, dunk both of them in the center bowl that's filled with warm water.

Wait a second....

Is the water in that center bowl warm, or is it really hot...or is it really cold...OR is it both???

Though you yourself know better, one hand is telling you it's hot water and the other hand is telling you it feels like cold water. And, interestingly, it should be the right hand that says "hot" and the left that says "cold," exactly the opposite of the water they were just soaking in!

Know why this is happening? Well, just like the optical illusion in which you thought you were seeing a hole in your hand, your brain is getting conflicting signals here. Because "hot" and "cold" are relative terms, what you experience depends on your point of reference. Your right hand was using the cold water it was just soaking in as a reference, and your left hand was using the hot water for its comparison. Now, when you put both hands in the warm water, you're working with two different sets of reference points. In the most literal sense, you can now say you're "running hot and cold!"

BUBBLE TROUBLE!

Perhaps you've heard of a little thing called BUBBLE GUM? Yes, we're talking about that totally delicious, un-nutritious novelty that keeps you chewing all day long.

Just in case you never learned the proper way to blow a bubble, here's a quick lesson: stick the gum in your mouth and chew it for a few minutes to make sure it's nice and soft. After the gum has gotten to the totally stretchy stage, flatten it between your tongue and front teeth. Now open your teeth slightly and use your tongue to start pushing the gum out between them. Since the tip of your tongue is rounded, it's going to help the gum take on a spherical shape to form a good-looking bubble. Slowly, start blowing through the gum until the bubble begins to form. When it has achieved a good size, clamp your teeth down at the end of it, so you seal the air inside.

Easy, right? A snap, so to speak!

Okay, now **let's see if you can blow a second bubble inside the first one**. The same bubble-making rules apply; except you might want to be chewing *two* pieces of gum instead of one and try to make the first bubble you blow a little bigger than normal. Once you've blown it and sealed it, there will still be some extra gum material between your front teeth. This is what you're going to use to form the interior bubble.

 So, as best you can, knead the remaining gum in your mouth until you've managed to flatten it against your front teeth. Now put your tongue to it and slowly start blowing into it. Since you already have a large bubble blocking the new bubble's way, the only place it can expand into is inside that first bubble. Assuming you can keep the first one from popping, you'll now have a little bubble inside the original one. And if you get really good in the bubble-making process, you can continue to blow bubbles inside bubbles until you run out of gum!

You Did It!!!

Congratulations! You actually got through an entire book filled with supposedly impossible tasks—and you got through like a champion.

Know what that means? **YOU RULE!**

Hopefully, by going through these challenges and tricks, you picked up some cool new skills and mastered things you previously thought were absolutely undoable. In the process, we also hoped you learned that, oftentimes, breaking a skill down into small, manageable chunks makes it easier to accomplish. Of course, this is not *always* going to work, and occasionally there will be things that are truly impossible to do, but it's important for you to realize that hard work, patience, and practice will help you through a lot of tricky situations and seemingly difficult things to do.

The bottom line is that you're a born **survivor** and the more things you try, the more things you'll succeed in doing. It's just like how the expression goes:

"**You gotta be in it to win it**, and you can't win unless you play!"